KANSAS

Kit Carson

Bent's Old Fort
Nat'l. Monument

Lamar

Las Animas

Arkans...

Springfield

OKLAHOMA

TEXAS

Clayton

287 385

54

287 385

987 385

40 287

24

State Capitol

Colorado Springs

Pueblo

La Junta

50

25

WITHDRAWN

64 18

Canadian River

Conchas
Reservoir

Raton

25

Old Opera
House

Cañon City

160

Great Sand Dunes
Nat'l Monument

Walsenburg

Trinidad

64

Taos

Santa Fe

Sangre de Cristo Mountains

Alamosa

159

Rio Grande

NEW MEXICO

592

285 68

Leadville

Buena Vista

Salida

17

Rio Grande

...delier
...l. Mon.

M O U N T A I N s

Mt. Elbert
14.433 ft

Gunnison

Saguache

Del Norte

80

Redstone

Aspen

Curecanti Nat'l.
Recreation Area

Pagosa
Springs

Navajo
Reservoir

D1530729

60

50

Black Canyon of
The Gunnison
Nat'l. Mon.

N

40

Cleveholm
Manor

Fruita

Grand
Junction

Delta

50

Montrose

550

Silverton

Telluride

Durango

160

Farmington

Chaco Culture
Nat'l Historic
Park

20

Distance in miles

Colorado
National
Monument

50

Strater
Hotel

Mesa Verde
Nat'l Park

Cortez

0

666

40

Gallup

...iver

CAROL M. HIGHSMITH AND TED LANDPHAIR

COLORADO

A PHOTOGRAPHIC TOUR

CRESCENT BOOKS

NEW YORK

PAGE 1: The Santa Fe Trail, the nine-hundred-mile-long trading route through southeastern Colorado from Missouri into Mexican territory at Santa Fe, was once littered with the bones of many animals that did not survive the harsh journey. Alongside the trail, buffalo were hunted nearly to extinction. The "green ocean" of the monotonous plains is not without its moments of splendor. PAGES 2–3: Sunsets are stunning. Before electricity, windmills dotted the horizon, pulling up precious water for humans and beasts alike. Here and in most parts of Colorado, there was rarely a paucity of wind to turn them.

This 1997 edition is published by Crescent Books, a division of Random House Value Publishing, Inc., 201 East 50th Street, New York, N.Y. 10022.

Crescent Books and colophon are trademarks of Random House Value Publishing, Inc.

Random House
New York • Toronto • London • Sydney • Auckland
http://www.randomhouse.com/

Printed and bound in China

Library of Congress Cataloging-in-Publication Data
Highsmith, Carol M., 1946–
Colorado / Carol M. Highsmith and Ted Landphair.
    p.   cm. — (A photographic tour)
ISBN 0-517-18608-x (hc: alk. paper)
1. Colorado—Tours. 2. Colorado—Pictorial works. 3. Colorado—Description and travel.
I. Landphair, Ted, 1942–   . II. Title. III. Series.
F774.3.H54   1997   97–12748
917.8804´33—dc21   CIP

8   7   6   5   4   3   2   1

Designed by Robert L. Wiser, Archetype Press, Inc., Washington, D.C.

All photographs by Carol M. Highsmith unless otherwise credited:
map by XNR Productions, page 5
painting by Charles H. Harmon (courtesy of Colorado Springs Fine Arts Center), page 6
Buffalo Bill Memorial Museum, pages 8 and 21
Russell Johnson Collection, pages 9 and 11
Overland Trail Museum (Sterling), page 10
City of Greeley Museums, pages 12 and 13
Colorado Springs Fine Arts Center, page 14
Swearingen family (Pueblo), page 15
Denver Public Library Western History Department, page 16
Robert C. Bishop, page 17
Molly Brown House (Historic Denver, Inc.), pages 18 and 19
Brown Palace Hotel, page 20

THE AUTHORS GRATEFULLY ACKNOWLEDGE THE SERVICES, ACCOMMODATIONS, AND SUPPORT PROVIDED BY
HILTON HOTELS CORPORATION
AND
THE BRECKENRIDGE HILTON RESORT
THE DENVER HILTON SOUTH, ENGLEWOOD
THE GRAND JUNCTION HILTON
IN CONNECTION WITH THE COMPLETION OF THIS BOOK.

THE AUTHORS ALSO WISH TO THANK THE FOLLOWING FOR THEIR GENEROUS ASSISTANCE AND HOSPITALITY DURING THEIR VISITS TO COLORADO:

Floyd Ciruli, President, Ciruli Associates Research and Public Policy, Denver
David Halaas, Chief Historian, Colorado Historical Society, Denver
Colorado Travel & Tourism Authority, Englewood Kelly Ladyga, Director of Communications
Denver Metro Convention & Visitors Bureau Joy Long, Public Relations Manager
Pikes Peak Country Attractions Association, Manitou Springs Amy Pannell, Promotions Manager
Aileen Berlin Barry, President, Advertising Images, Inc., Greeley
Durango! Area Chamber Resort Association Patti Zink, Media Relations Director
Northeast Colorado Travel Region Trish Lengel, West Yuma County Chamber of Commerce, Yuma
Mary Stewart, Sterling, Colorado
Pueblo Chamber of Commerce Erin Hergert, Communications Director
Fort Morgan Area Chamber of Commerce Cathy Schull, Executive Director
Abriendo Inn, Pueblo Kerrelyn Trent, Inkeeper
The German House Bed & Breakfast Inn, Greeley Detlef and Celia Scholl, Innkeepers
Hearthstone Inn, Manitou Springs Dot Williams, Innkeeper
Mountain View Bed & Breakfast, Dolores Brenda Dunn, Innkeeper
The Rochester Hotel and The Leland House Bed & Breakfast Suites, Durango Kirk Komick, Innkeeper
Mesa Verde Company, Mesa Verde National Park, Mancos Curtis W. Smart, Transportation Manager
Denver Center for the Performing Arts Constance Harvey, Associate Director, Media Relations
The Buckhorn Exchange Restaurant, Denver

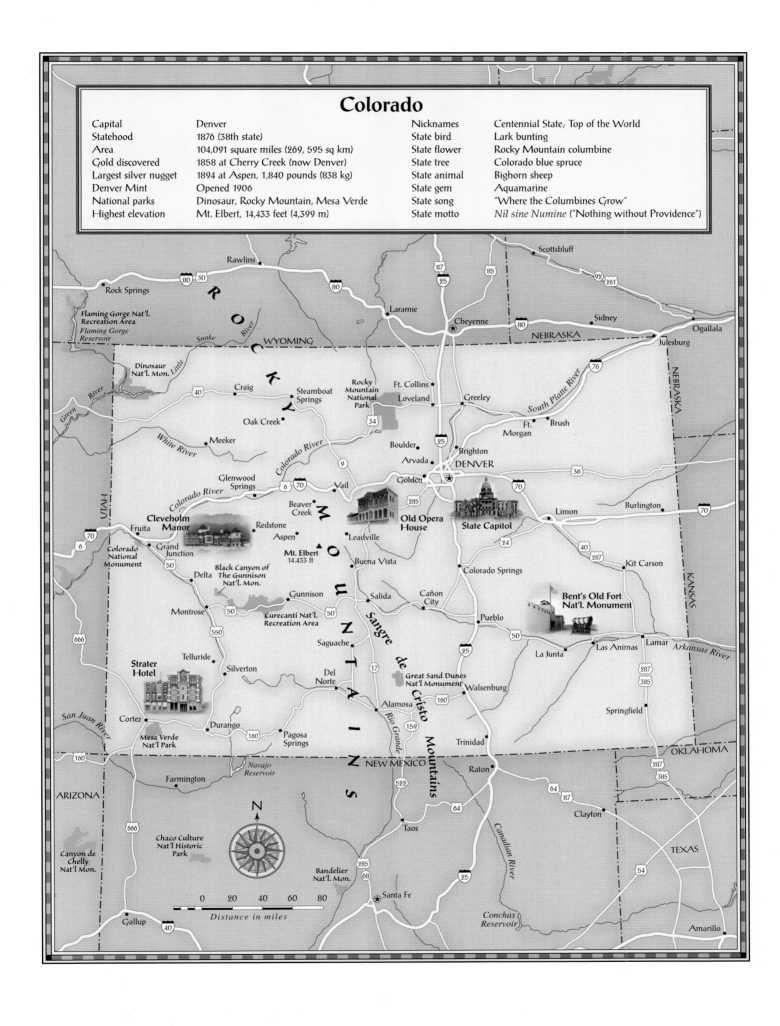

Colorado

Capital	Denver	Nicknames	Centennial State; Top of the World
Statehood	1876 (38th state)	State bird	Lark bunting
Area	104,091 square miles (269, 595 sq km)	State flower	Rocky Mountain columbine
Gold discovered	1858 at Cherry Creek (now Denver)	State tree	Colorado blue spruce
Largest silver nugget	1894 at Aspen, 1,840 pounds (838 kg)	State animal	Bighorn sheep
Denver Mint	Opened 1906	State gem	Aquamarine
National parks	Dinosaur, Rocky Mountain, Mesa Verde	State song	"Where the Columbines Grow"
Highest elevation	Mt. Elbert, 14,433 feet (4,399 m)	State motto	*Nil sine Numine* ("Nothing without Providence")

Rawlins

Scottsbluff

Rock Springs

ROCKY

Flaming Gorge Nat'l. Recreation Area
Flaming Gorge Reservoir

Laramie

Cheyenne

NEBRASKA

Sidney

Ogallala

Julesburg

WYOMING

Snake River

Dinosaur Nat'l. Mon.

Little

Green River

Craig

White River

Meeker

Steamboat Springs

Oak Creek

Rocky Mountain National Park

Ft. Collins

Loveland

Greeley

South Platte River

Ft. Morgan

Brush

NEBRASKA

Boulder

Arvada

DENVER

Brighton

Colorado River

Glenwood Springs

Vail

Golden

Limon

Burlington

UTAH

Colorado River

Beaver Creek

Old Opera House

State Capitol

Cleveholm Manor

Redstone

Aspen

Leadville

Fruita

Colorado National Monument

Grand Junction

Mt. Elbert 14.433 ft

Buena Vista

Colorado Springs

Kit Carson

KANSAS

Delta

Black Canyon of The Gunnison Nat'l. Mon.

Gunnison

Salida

Cañon City

Bent's Old Fort Nat'l. Monument

Montrose

Curecanti Nat'l. Recreation Area

Pueblo

Saguache

La Junta

Las Animas

Lamar

Arkansas River

Strater Hotel

Telluride

Silverton

Del Norte

Great Sand Dunes Nat'l Monument

Walsenburg

Springfield

Cortez

Durango

Pagosa Springs

Alamosa

Rio Grande

Trinidad

OKLAHOMA

Mesa Verde Nat'l Park

San Juan River

Navajo Reservoir

NEW MEXICO

Raton

ARIZONA

Farmington

Clayton

TEXAS

Chaco Culture Nat'l Historic Park

N

Taos

Canyon de Chelly Nat'l Mon.

Bandelier Nat'l. Mon.

Santa Fe

Conchas Reservoir

Gallup

0   20   40   60   80
Distance in miles

Amarillo

MOUNTAINS

Sangre de Cristo Mountains

COLORADO SHIMMERS IN THE FALL, when the lemon sun shines through the thin air, backlighting yellow and gold aspens on ten thousand hillsides. It astounds in the winter, when America's highest state, nearly seven thousand feet *on average,* sparkles under blankets of snow. And it's a feast for the senses in spring and summer, when evergreens glimmer against a stormy afternoon sky, streams hurry down from the Continental Divide into meadows filled with wildflowers, and mountain zephyrs refresh the air. The state's eastern high plains, western plateau, and central Rockies harbor bear and elk, bison and beaver, coyotes and mountain lions that first lured hunters and trappers there—and also all manner of predatory birds, whitewater trout, and woodland snakes.

Colorado is a state of incredible contradictions. It was among the wildest parts of the West, yet places like Denver were almost instant cities, copied from eastern models to supply the gold camps and railroads. Thus they were surprisingly genteel. Colorado is part of the vast, open West—what one author called the nation's "Empty Quarter"—yet its Front Range, on the eastern foothills of the Rocky Mountains, is a virtual strip city from Fort Collins, near the Wyoming border, 150 miles south to Pueblo. Ninety percent of the state's population lives there, more than 2.1 million people in metropolitan Denver alone. The population of the five-county region in and around Denver doubled between 1960 and 1992, and new Colorado housing permits topped forty thousand a year through most of the 1990s. In the curious synergy that comes with growth, all the new people helped create new jobs, especially in construction and service industries.

And Colorado has certainly been eager to grow. Many towns gave industries deep subsidies to move there and passed bond measures to build highways and other infrastructure improvements to grease the way. The state built the world's largest airport, Denver International, in the 1990s specifically to attract more trade, industrial development, and jobs. It gave lucrative tax incentives to high-tech companies to locate in the state; these companies, in turn, attracted tens of thousands of Californians, Texans, and others who had lost work or were fed up with their lifestyles elsewhere. While Coloradans once flaunted bumper stickers that read "Don't Californiate Colorado" and joked that it would be great to discourage prospective newcomers by posting billboards urging "Think Salt Lake. Try Ogden. Have you seen Vegas?"—they met the growth of the 1990s with resignation, investing heavily in new highways, light rail, sports facilities, schools, and libraries to accommodate the influx.

Though it was inexorably growing, Colorado was also trying to limit growth that would spoil the very beauty that attracted newcomers in the first place. As part of the state's "Smart Growth" program in the early 1990s, voters approved spending all of the state's lottery proceeds on the purchase and preservation of open space. Cities like Boulder placed tough new moratoriums on development and worked harder at preserving tracts of prairie and foothills. The state even did away with its tourism-promotion board, figuring the word had been amply spread that Colorado was a wonderful place to be.

It's been said that the new arrivals are notorious for their "last person in closes the door" attitudes toward further growth. But responding to statewide poll after poll, Coloradans rate the state's quality of life high, the beauty of the mountains unsurpassed, the appeal of easy access to outdoor recreational opportunities irresistible, and the benefits that newcomers bring—such as improved restaurants, cultural activities, and sports—worth most of the headaches that come with them. Every second Coloradan owns a four-wheel-drive sport-utility vehicle, and the local

Landscape artist Charles H. Harmon caught the luminescent quality of the Rocky Mountains in this untitled 1890 study. Colorado's thin air, rumbling mountain storms, and top-of-the-world vistas seemingly so close to the sun, can turn craggy hillsides a myriad of colors in a single day.

For four months in 1885, Buffalo Bill Cody made his friend Sitting Bull, the Sioux leader at the Battle of Little Big Horn, a star of his Wild West show. Buffalo Bill is buried near Denver.

joke is that the other half own motor homes. Or so it would seem when one is caught in a Sunday-evening traffic jam coming out of the mountains. Dirt roads, and places with no roads at all, have thus been opened to easy exploration. Picnicking in a mountain meadow, or frolicking on a glacial outcropping, has become part of everyday life. Of course, this also threatens the very beauty, and the wildlife, that many set off to find.

The state's parallel courses—toward conservation as well as growth—are well illustrated in Pitkin County, south of Glenwood Springs and Vail in the Central Rockies. A few miles south of Interstate 70, the road out of Glenwood Springs forks. One tine, State Route 82, winds through Snowmass and Aspen on its way to the spectacular Independence Pass. It was at Aspen in 1946 that the world's longest chairlift opened. Prospectors in the area had once used "Norwegian snowshoes" to search for ore. Miners, mail carriers, and even ministers learned to ski using homemade wooden skis and a single pole. The U.S. Tenth Mountain Division, which fought the German Army in the alpine passes of Italy during World War II, trained at nearby Camp Hale, and many returned to the Aspen area to continue their skiing once the Aspen Skiing Company began operations. At the same time, Chicago industrialist Walter Paepcke and his wife, Elizabeth, founded a covey of vibrant cultural institutions loosely called the "Aspen Idea." These included the Aspen Institute for Humanistic Studies, the International Design Conference at Aspen, and the Aspen Music School. Today the valley is crammed with ski resorts and chalets, fine restaurants, and sophisticated shops.

The array of services and outdoor activities is so vast at an Aspen or Vail or Copper Mountain that thousands of retirees have moved there. They are looking for full-scale developments offering numerous amenities, not necessarily ski resorts; some don't even ski. By 1997, Colorado ranked third in the nation in number of new retirees entering the state each year. Winters, they had discovered, were not as long or harsh as the occasional blizzard makes them seem; Colorado's road system is excellent; and rural mountain communities, in particular, offer those with a decent nest egg real-estate bargains and an unpressured environment of fishing, golf, and nature walks. Appropriately, given its number of high-mountain aeries, Colorado has also become a mecca for "lone eagles"—men and women whose professions enable them to telecommute without even venturing into an office.

It was not tourism that first brought white settlers to these high mountains. Except for the Santa Fe Trail that skirted south into New Mexico, most great migration routes and early railroads bypassed Colorado's spine of peaks along the Continental Divide altogether, in favor of more hospitable passes in Wyoming. The Spanish, who had moved north out of Mexico and claimed much of what is today the southern half of Colorado, simply stopped when they reached the Rockies, leaving the mountains to the Utes and Shoshones. Not just the imposing peaks deterred them. Marshall Sprague pointed out in a U.S. Bicentennial book on Colorado that the Spanish custom of forcing native Indians to build the Spaniards' pueblos and work their farms held them up as well. Noted Sprague, "The [San Luis] valley was used only by the fierce plains Comanches and mountain Utes, nomadic horse Indians who prized their freedom to roam and refused to be held on some Spanish hacienda to plant corn and beans." Besides, the high country's growing season was so short that early explorers had to either shoot and catch their food, or carry it in. So it was at the San Luis Valley that the Spanish stopped their expansion of "Colorado"—Spanish for "red," a name they first applied to a river that runs through the region.

It was gold—and eventually silver—that opened the high country to settlement and began a boom and bust cycle (later tied to oil, uranium, and agriculture as well) that would bedevil the state for generations. John Babsone Lane Soule, a Terre Haute, Indiana, newspaperman—not Horace Greeley—first wrote the words "Go west, young man" in 1851. But Greeley, the astute editor of the *New York Tribune*, journeyed west himself, to Denver eight years later. He came away musing about the "intoxication of success" in the Colorado goldfields, surely to be followed by "the valley of humiliation. Each season will see thousands turn away disappointed, only to give place to other thousands, sanguine and eager as if none had ever failed."

At the time of Greeley's visit, the little community of Cripple Creek, high in the mountains west of Manitou Springs, was little more than a supply center for a big cattle ranch. But in 1891 a cowboy, Bob Womack, discovered gold in Poverty Gulch. Within a year, twenty-five hundred people lived in Cripple Creek; four years later, the population had swollen to ten thousand; and at the turn of the century, it was Colorado's fourth-largest city, with elegant homes, two opera houses, its own stock exchange, seventy-three saloons, and a population of twenty-five thousand. Five hundred mines pulled an average of $20 million in gold out of the hills each year. Then came an inevitable decline—with closed mines and a dwindling population that fell below one thousand by 1950. Because Cripple Creek is far from an interstate highway or even a main U.S. route, it seemed fated to become another ghost town. Whether limited gaming will prove to bring a long-term "boom" back to the area remains to be seen.

Boom and bust cycles were not confined to the mines. More than twenty-five thousand

Trees were scarce in northeastern Colorado. Pioneers built homes and refuges from Indian attacks out of rocks and sod. This was Overland Trail country, along the South Platte River. Another route west, the Oregon Trail, followed the North Platte.

Point of Rocks View Near Sterling Colo

people were employed in oil and gas statewide in the 1970s, and Denver's skyline exploded with more than twenty million square feet of new office space owned by or leased to energy-related companies. When independent multimillionaire producer Marvin Davis sold off most of his petroleum production in 1981, it presaged an unforgettable economic downturn. A year later, Exxon abandoned its Colony Oil Shale project in western Colorado, scuttling an investment of nearly a billion dollars. By 1988, more than fourteen thousand petroleum jobs had disappeared. While the state partially rebounded, the energy crisis provoked a statewide determination to break the yo-yo nature of its economic fortunes. Before long, government and business together had committed to building a new international airport as the major economic "port" of the Mountain West; offering incentives to bring new—and especially high-tech—jobs into the state; and protecting the state's most visible asset, its stunningly beautiful environment, at all costs, while seeking this growth. The strategy succeeded beyond its planners' wildest dreams, to the point that officials grew edgy about some of the consequences (like congestion) and breathed a secret sigh of relief in 1996 when figures showed that the state, while still growing, had slowed the rate a bit.

The United States first got its hands on part of Colorado in the Louisiana Purchase of 1803. Incredibly, Louisiana stretched that far west, and as far north as the Canadian border. The French paid little attention to the high country of Colorado, however, other than to dispatch a few trappers, in part because of rival Spain's presence directly to the south. Nor had any known American ever even seen the Colorado portion of these vast new holdings. When an American expedition, under Captain Zebulon Pike, first spied the Rocky Mountains in the distance, Pike assumed they must be about the same height as the eastern Appalachians. The Rockies proved, of course, to

Oxen Passing Through Sterling Colo.

Even as Sterling was growing and mechanizing, oxen and draft horses were plentiful on the beet and alfalfa farms outside town. Note the long, ready whip in the hand of the oxen's herder.

be three or even four times higher. Pike and his sixteen men trudged all through the mountains, looking for the source of the Arkansas and Red rivers (they never found them), and more than once had to hike many miles around precipitous canyons like the Royal Gorge on the Arkansas. In an ultimate indignity following a harrowing winter in the mountains, the men came upon a squad of Spanish soldiers, who arrested the Americans and hauled them off to jail seven hundred miles away in Chihuahua. All would eventually be released.

In 1821, Mexico gained its independence from Spain, and the new government opened trade with the United States through what is now Southeast Colorado. Soon two branches of the Santa Fe Trail between Missouri and Mexico passed through Colorado. "Mountain men" like Jim Bridger were some of the first to veer off from the trail in search of animals to trap for their fur. Tales of these men and the country they tamed thrilled their countrymen back east and gave Americans their first inkling of the wonders that lay beyond the prairie. Before long the fur trade was connecting remote reaches of the high Colorado mountains with the most fashionable salons of London and Paris. "All of this Unorganized Territory west of Missouri had no government whatsoever," wrote Marshall Sprague. "The Bent brothers [who had built a fort that became a medieval-style city on the Arkansas River] were the law, acting as judges and sheriffs in keeping peace among the Indians and travelers on the Santa Fe Trail."

In the 1840s, U.S. Senator Thomas Hart Benton of Missouri, whose dreams of American expansion to the Pacific were couched in the term "Manifest Destiny," prodded the U.S. Army into organizing a scouting and military reconnaissance expedition under Lieutenant John Charles Frémont, who happened to be the senator's son-in-law. Frémont was determined to find a more direct way west than the roundabout Oregon Trail. His wife, Jessie, went along,

So handy was Ivan "Jack" Elliot with a horse and lariat that he toured England with a Colorado rodeo. Elliot, a Greeley rancher, furnished much of the stock for Cheyenne, Wyoming's, famous Frontier Days.

sending back colorful dispatches that further romanticized the adventure. The Frémont expedition barged throughout the Front Range, near the present-day sites of Denver, Manitou Springs, and Pueblo. The party ran into Kit Carson, who guided them north into Wyoming, from where they found their way to California before heading home through northern Mexico. Frémont would lead two more forays through the Rockies, but it was his wife's accounts of the first expedition through that lofty wilderness that ignited everyday Americans' interest and refueled Benton's determination to push the Spanish and British out of the "American" West. Brigham Young and his band of Mormons, who were enduring persecution in downstate Illinois, even studied Jessie Frémont's accounts as a guide to searching out a new kingdom beyond Colorado. Soon thousands of Americans were pressing westward. In 1847, after the Mexican government protested the annexation of Texas, President Polk declared war on Mexico, and an army of seventeen hundred men under General Stephen Kearney marched to Santa Fe and took that provincial capital without firing a shot. He would go on to conquer California as well; a year later, Mexico relinquished its entire Northwest (our Southwest) to the United States. Included was the former Spanish portion of what would become Colorado.

Officially, however, there was still no such place. Parts of it were in Utah Territory, one sliver was contained in an extension of the Texas Panhandle, and the east and middle were split between Kansas Territory to the south and Nebraska Territory to the north. Kansas was rent by bloody fighting over the slavery issue—a preview of the Civil War to come—and many families fled to remote Arapahoe County in the Colorado region to escape it. At the same time, gold prospectors who had tapped out in California showed up there as well. Many of these people sent back even more incredible tales of "Pikes Peak," spurring more migration. When bits of placer gold were discovered at the juncture of the South Platte River and Cherry Creek near what today is downtown Denver, cries of "Pikes Peak or Bust" were sounded across the nation. After a solid vein was discovered and the Central City boom ignited in 1859, more than fifty thousand starry-eyed prospectors poured into the region. A year earlier, with the rest of Kansas still embroiled in battle, soldiers who had come to establish formal government in Arapahoe County came upon a tiny settlement on Cherry Creek called St. Charles and renamed it "Denver" in honor of a former Kansas territorial governor. It was at Denver that citizens of the region declared a new, highly unofficial—even illegal—territory that they called "Jefferson." Hoping to extricate themselves from Nebraska and Kansas's squabbles over slavery, they even elected a rump governor. The Jefferson name did not stick, however, and when seven southern states seceded from the Union in 1861, President Lincoln hastened to sweep this potentially rich mining country under Union protection by declaring "Colorado" an official U.S. territory by presidential proclamation. Drafters had laid out an almost perfect rectangle that adjoined parts of seven states, without even knowing what was "out there" in many of the far-western reaches of the territory. At "Four Corners," Colorado's boundary intersected those of Utah, Arizona, and New Mexico territories. As the only spot in the nation where four states come together today, remote Four Corners remains a tourist curiosity.

The telegraph reached Denver in 1863, and railroads connected Front Range towns with

Cheyenne and the mighty Union Pacific Railroad in the decade to follow. (In 1870, a haughty Cheyenne newspaper sniggered that Denver was "too near to Cheyenne to ever amount to much.") Eastern Colorado became cowboy country, as herds of longhorns were driven up from Texas to fatten on buffalo grass before being shipped east by rail. With the discovery of silver in Southwest Colorado in 1868, the Utes, the last of Colorado's indigenous Native Americans, were forced off their land. On August 1, 1876, Colorado was admitted to the Union as the thirty-eighth state. It was less than a month past the one-hundredth anniversary of the nation's founding; hence the nickname "the Centennial State." Already accustomed to boom and bust cycles in the goldfields, Colorado struggled with drought and the overproduction of silver—which was eventually devalued, ruining thousands of mine owners, investors, and miners. With the advent of massive government irrigation projects in the early twentieth century, eastern Colorado sugar beet farmers found prosperity again. And the state's vast coal reserves fueled a giant steel mill in Pueblo and factories throughout the West. In 1941, the book *Colorado: America's Highest State*, researched by the Federal Writers' Project during the Depression, reported: "The State that stirred the pulsebeats of the continent with its tales of fortunes dug out of the rock and cowboys riding the range has more white-collar boys behind desks and girls behind store counters than hardy adventurers prospecting the hills." In the map printed inside the front and rear covers of the book, there was no Vail, no Aspen, no Telluride or Snowmass. Hardy adventurers came to see Pikes Peak, the Royal Gorge, and the Garden of the Gods, not to ski. By 1969, the state's largest employment segment was government service, including more than forty-four thousand federal workers. This re-emphasized the state's reliance upon natural resources and the environment for much of its well-being.

Volunteers from Greeley's five "hose companies" kept in shape in tournaments that featured hook-and-ladder races, footraces, and ladder-climbing competitions. Note the men's athletic outfits and the championship ribbons pinned upon them.

Forty-nine years after Spencer Penrose opened the Broadmoor Hotel in Colorado Springs, students from the resort's art academy sketch among the vivid red rocks of the Garden of the Gods in 1920.

In its first few years, Denver, the state capital and by far its largest city, survived a flood, widespread fires, several Indian attacks, and even an invading force of Confederates from Texas during the Civil War. With the discovery of gold in the mountains, Denver became a boomtown of saloons, gambling halls, and wagon trains lining its muddy streets. At the beginning of the twentieth century, some of the wealth of the mountains was poured into mansions on Pennsylvania Street, turning Denver into the most elegant city between Saint Louis and San Francisco. Consumptives from all over the world showed up as well, convinced that the high, dry air would relieve their tuberculosis. Tourists arrived with copies of dime novels by the American Zane Gray and the German Karl May in hand. Colorado's narrow-gauge and short-line railroads hired photographers and artists to create glowing promotional campaigns touting mining towns that had gone bust but in which the railroads still had interests.

These were the days of Molly Brown, born Margaret Tobin in Hannibal, Missouri. She married J. J. Brown, who had struck it rich in the mines of Leadville. The Browns bought a lava-stone mansion built in Denver by architect William Lang. While Molly schemed to maneuver the family into the city's snooty society register, J. J. longed for the simple life back home. Eventually they separated; J. J. returned to Leadville, and Molly began extensive world travels. She became a national heroine when she caught a ride on the inaugural voyage of the S.S. *Titanic;* when the boat struck an iceberg, she used her knowledge of several languages to direct many women and children to safety, and took charge of a lifeboat when a crewman became paralyzed with fear as the great ship sank. Her story became the basis for the Broadway musical *The Unsinkable Molly Brown.* The Browns' house is now a museum, run by the private, nonprofit Historic Denver, Incorporated.

At a time when adventurers were flocking to Denver on the way to the camps to seek their fortunes—or returning to the city with fortunes in hand—a carpenter-turned-entrepreneur named Henry Cordes Brown was building his "Palace Hotel." Brown, who donated the land for the state capitol and made his fortune selling off other acres of the city's Capitol Hill, commissioned Frank E. Edbrooke to design his grand hotel. The Colorado red granite and Arizona sandstone hotel, adorned on its seventh-floor façade with twenty-six carved medallions depicting native Rocky Mountain animals, included the nation's first atrium lobby. The triangular Brown Palace has been open every minute of every day since it opened in 1892. The city's art museum, botanic gardens, and museum of natural history are world famous, and Denver became a world-class sports town with the arrival of the National Hockey League Avalanche to join the football Broncos, baseball Rockies, and basketball Nuggets.

Denver's two newspapers, the *Post* and the *Rocky Mountain News*, fought a brutal circulation war for supremacy in the 1990s in one of the nation's last two-daily cities. The *Post* maintained a strategy of saturating the state, as well as parts of Wyoming, New Mexico, and Kansas, while the *News* concentrated its efforts on Denver and other Front Range cities, canceling deliveries over the Rockies. In the early days of the twentieth century, more than ten thousand electric lights illuminated Curtis Street's thirteen legitimate theaters, whose marquees could be seen far out on the prairie. The stock-market crash of 1929 and the Great Depression that followed doomed most of these ventures, and for decades the city seemed too consumed by other matters to bother with culture. But in the late 1980s, a nonprofit group called the Denver Center for the Performing Arts turned an area of urban decay around Curtis and Fourteenth streets into the largest cultural entertainment complex outside New York City. Today it includes the historic Auditorium Theatre (where William Jennings Bryan was once nominated for president), a former police building (now the administrative offices), a concert hall, and complex of six separate theaters. All are entered beneath an eighty-foot-high, block-long glass arch.

There's incredible art in a surprising place outside Denver as well. Denver's $4.3-billion International Airport (DIA) features the largest public-art program in American history. Its roofline of thirty-four peaks—symbolizing snowy Rocky Mountain tops—has become one of the world's most recognizable architectural symbols. The airport, which can land one hundred planes an hour in weather that would have closed the old Stapleton Field, covers fifty-three square miles of eastern Colorado prairie—twice the size of Manhattan Island. So massive was the DIA construction project that Colorado cities like Pueblo actually postponed their own construction plans almost two years because of the shortage of skilled labor, which was otherwise occupied at the giant airport.

In 1917, Denver author Dabney Otis Collins wrote, "When I walk down a Denver street, I always feel as if I were listening to a brass band." With its Victorian buildings reflecting in the mirrored glass of downtown skyscrapers, the horse-drawn carriages along Larimer Square, and views of snow-capped peaks at the end of Seventeenth Street, the feeling is palpable today as well. Stand on the fifteenth step on the west side of the State Capitol—modeled after the U.S. version in Washington—and you are exactly 5,280 feet above sea level in the "Mile High City." The building is best known for its brilliant dome, covered in two hundred ounces of twenty-four-carat gold. But its truly

Until 1874, residents of Pueblo purchased their water in barrels at twenty-five cents apiece. Afterward, many families held onto the casks to catch rainwater. Two Swearingen brothers used theirs for sheer fun.

Steel magnate Cleve Osgood built the Redstone Inn as the centerpiece of his coke workers' "company town" in the Redstone Valley. His bachelor foremen and visitors to his sumptuous Cleveholm Castle residence stayed there.

priceless material is the Colorado onyx used inside as wainscoting. The entire world supply of this rose-colored stone was used in the building, and no more of it has ever been found. Down the street at the Colorado History Museum is a huge model of the city as it appeared in 1860—before it was twice destroyed, once by fire and once by flood. The United States Mint, also downtown, is the nation's second-largest storehouse of gold bullion. More than one million bricks and sixty-thousand cubic feet of granite went into erecting the 1904 structure. More than five billion coins are minted here each year, and its floor is virtually covered with trays, sacks, and conveyor belts full of brilliant, flashing coins. Denver's Museum of Western Art features more than 125 paintings and sculptures by such Western masters as Frederic Remington, Charles Russell, Thomas Moran, Albert Bierstadt, and Georgia O'Keefe. There's a Black American West Museum and Heritage Center as well, housed in the former home of pioneer physician Justina Ford. The museum has a cowboy room, military displays—including information on the African-American "Buffalo Soldiers"—and oral histories.

Metropolitan Denver also boasts a delicious tourist attraction—its beer. Coors Brewery, in suburban Golden, is the largest single brewery on earth, producing more than seventeen million barrels of beer a year. And Downtown Denver is home to fifteen brewpubs and microbreweries, concocting forty different local beers.

Colorado seems determined to keep its big city vital. Though suburban Jefferson County for the first time edged Denver in number of registered voters in the mid-1990s, most of the metro area's big law firms, service companies, cultural institutions, and sports facilities have remained in the core city. Even the brown haze that once seemed to hang perpetually overhead, obscuring the beautiful mountains, was ameliorated by tighter automobile-emission

standards and the introduction of oxidated fuels. In 1996, for the first time since federal air-quality standards took effect two decades previously, Denver went through an entire year with no violations.

The images most associated with Colorado—mountains, snow, skiing, clean air—certainly still fit, despite the state's spate of growth. If anything, the mountain passes and rushing brooks can be even more spectacular in person than a tourist brochure can describe. And surprises are abundant. How many Americans realize that the eastern third of the state is as flat as Kansas—and was in fact part of Kansas's Arapahoe County prior to statehood—with cattle feed lots, rail yards, rodeo arenas, and miles of telephone poles stretching to the horizon? Or that the famous Santa Fe Trail, once the haunt of Kit Carson and other western legends, winds through Southeast Colorado on its way to New Mexico? Remnants of the days of Spanish conquistadors and missionaries remain in South Central Colorado's San Luis Valley—so much so that many phrases are taken from "Spain Spanish," rather than the Mexican dialect. One does not need to venture into the high mountains to see incredible rock formations. The Garden of the Gods, in the valley below Pikes Peak near Colorado Springs, has ribbons of red rock reminiscent of southern Utah, and the Western Plateau holds secrets like Grand Mesa, a giant tabletop that extends for miles. Gambling resorts have transformed obscure little mountain towns like Cripple Creek, Black Hawk, and Central City into lively tour-bus destinations. Twenty-eight percent of state gaming proceeds is earmarked for the State Historical Society, which uses the money—well over eight million dollars a year in the 1990s—to save, restore, and even find historic sites. Pikes Peak, the state's most famous mountain because of the Zebulon Pike expedition that brought back news of Colorado's grandeur—and because of the incredible engineering

The peacefulness of the mountains was one lure of the Colorado Chautauqua in Boulder. So were tub-thumping speeches, hikes, and motivational lectures. Women and children predominated; most men stayed at work.

feat that resulted in completion of a paved road winding around the mountainside to the summit—is nowhere near the highest peak in the state. In fact, it ranks toward the middle of the fifty-four peaks over fourteen thousand feet high. But Pikes Peak sticks in one's memory because it sits relatively apart from other mountains, looming over Colorado Springs and a picturesque valley.

Colorado's single most frequented attraction is Rocky Mountain National Park, north and west of Denver. Opened in 1915 and staffed by National Park Service rangers, the park, which straddles the Continental Divide and contains seventy-eight peaks twelve thousand feet high and above, hosts around three million visitors annually. The mountain village of Grand Lake, on the park's western boundary, is one of Colorado's oldest resort communities. So is nearby Hot Sulphur Springs, which attracted tourists early in the twentieth century and was the site of Colorado's first skiing and jumping hills. Today, Grand County is Colorado's "Dude Ranch Capital" and one of the state's richest sanctuaries for elk, deer, mountain lions, bald eagles, and bears. It is also the site of one of Colorado's most colorful sporting events—the annual Grand County Rendezvous, a sled-dog race at Granby Sports Park involving more than 120 teams from across the nation.

Denver millionaire James Joseph "J. J." Brown made a fortune overnight in the mines of Leadville. He married the irrepressible Molly Brown, but longed for the humbler life of Leadville and eventually returned there.

Winter Park in Grand County is one of more than twenty thriving downhill skiing destinations—and uncounted hundreds of breathtaking cross-country trails—for which Colorado has become famous. The state boasts light, fluffy "champagne powder" snow, made possible by the generally dry air. There are more than twenty-five thousand acres of skiable terrain, 250 chair ski lifts (including more high-speed chairlifts than any other U.S. state), and an average of twenty-one feet of powder each season. And Colorado is sunnier than San Diego, Honolulu, or Miami Beach.

Colorado's high country is home to unforgettable towns like Idaho Springs, site of the Argo Gold Mill, where the Newhouse Tunnel bore through 4.7 miles of solid mountain rock to Central City, which for a time was "the Richest Square Mile on Earth." The mill cleaned, sorted, and processed the ore coming out of the Central City mines. These were uncivilized times, as evidenced by this notice in the *Idaho Springs Advance* of December 21, 1882:

The organization of the Independent Order of Perfected Inebriates is holding its own.

At the last regular meeting, charges preferred against J. Rackety Ledyard for being found in a beastly state of sobriety, were placed into the hands of the investigating committee.

Another little town, Georgetown, in Clear Creek County, became the "Silver Queen of the Rockies." Its Hotel de Paris, owned by Frenchman Louis Dupuy, advertised steam heat in 1875; and its Hamill House was home to one of Colorado's richest men. Filled with Victorian mansions and quaint storefronts, Georgetown has not needed gambling to draw crowds of tourists. Its shops and old hotels, loop steam railroad, silver mine tour, and scenic byway excursions through the majestic Guanella Pass draw visitors by the thousands. Another silver town, Leadville, is the jewel of the spectacular "Top of the Rockies" scenic tour past ghost towns, mines, and sheer drop-offs that seems more like a journey along the top of the world itself. Some of the area's high mountain passes put a lump in a driver's throat and beads of moisture on the palms. Mosquito Pass, for instance, at 13,186 feet, is suitable for four-wheel-drive vehicles only. It is the highest vehicular pass in America. Even the tame auto ride along Interstate 70 through Loveland Pass is a visual delight, tempered by long climbs and steep downhill grades and several sightings of "runaway truck" ramps.

The interstate finally begins a gradual descent toward Grand Junction, the state's western gateway and one of its most diverse destinations. Nearby are the stunning spires, massive domes, balanced rocks, and sheer-wall sandstone canyons of the Colorado National Monument. Grand Mesa, in this park, is the world's largest flat-topped mountain. "Masterpieces of erosion," the National Park Service calls them. The park owes its existence to John Otto of Grand Junction, who lived alone in the wild canyons, built miles of tortuous trails through them so others could appreciate their beauty, and enlisted hundreds of other citizens in a campaign to have the area declared a national park. He was rewarded in 1911 when just such a park was established. He was named caretaker but would accept only $1 a month to do the job over the next sixteen years. The Grand Junction area also features science hikes through Dinosaur Valley, where paleontologists have uncovered many stunning prehistoric fossils, a stop at the area's famous peach orchards, and a peek into the Black Canyon of the Gunnison, an awesome gorge formed by a 2,689-foot drop of the Gunnison River into a long, dark canyon.

Rivers running down from the Continental Divide cut the Western Slope's tablelands into a number of steep-sided, flat-topped hills besides Grand Mesa. Near the rim of Mesa Verde in Southwest Colorado, the prehistoric Anasazi built fortress homes, then disappeared only one hundred or so years after they had arrived. Since these cliff dwellers were relatively safe from enemies, it is thought that they simply moved south, joining with other native peoples, because of a string of harsh summers or winters that had exhausted their food supplies. Cliff Palace in the park is the largest known cliff dwelling in North America. Many of the clues about the daily lives of these Mesa Verde people come from their garbage heaps found down the slopes from their homes.

Nearby is one of Colorado's "hottest" cities—Durango—which is lined with Victorian homes and hotels and is the southern terminus of the narrow-gauge Silverton-to-Durango train. Over many decades, an estimated $300 million in gold and silver rode the train from the mines of the San Juan Mountains. Whitewater rafting on the nearby Animas River has become a favorite activity. The description of the experience, printed in a city news release, is cause enough for heart palpitations, without even taking the plunge:

Part of the time, you are just floating along enjoying the mountain scenery. You will discover gentle eddies where you can stop the raft, jump overboard, and swim for a while before resuming your journey. And sometimes, the river churns and gurgles part of the way like a bumpy four-wheel-drive road. Then suddenly, surrounded by churning holes of whitewater, you must dig in . . . and paddle like crazy.

For winter adventures, Telluride and Purgatory ski areas are not far away, and to the east, past Alamosa, is a geological curiosity, the Great Sand Dunes National Monument, the tallest sand dunes in

Once a farm girl, Molly Brown enjoyed social climbing in Denver and traveling the world with the Astors and other personages. "Unsinkable" Molly became a heroine during the Titanic *disaster in 1912.*

North America. They were built to heights of nearly seven hundred feet by fierce winds carrying billions of grains of sand across the San Luis Valley and depositing them at the foot of the Sangre de Cristo Mountains.

Colorado's most industrial city, Pueblo, lies on the western edge of Southeastern Colorado's scrubby Plains country, which was visited by Spanish conquistadors before the first English landed on Plymouth Rock. Some fields in the state's southeast corner have never felt the blade of a plow. Most of the land is unsuited to farming and susceptible to violent shifts in climate. Baking heat, blizzards, and violent winds are all common. One answer has been massive irrigation, but this produced serious drop-offs in water levels of the Arkansas and Platte (the Platte was already known as the river that is "a mile wide and an inch deep"). Colorado lost a lawsuit in which neighboring Kansas complained that the Centennial State was taking more than its share of flow from the river. The ruling in Kansas's favor meant some Colorado deep-water wells would have to be closed. Eastern Colorado had been home to the classic, nomadic Plains Indians—the Cheyenne, Arapaho, Lakota Sioux, Comanche, Pawnee, and Kiowas—all of whom hunted with varying degrees of cooperation and competition. Cattle ranches and a few tourist attractions like Bent's Old Fort on the Santa Fe Trail provide interesting diversions.

Colorado Springs, the state's second-largest city, lies between Pueblo and Denver along the Front Range. It was founded as a residential resort in the 1870s. Forty years later, it annexed Colorado City, which had been the first territorial capital. Colorado Springs and nearby Manitou Springs are home to one of the state's greatest concentrations of attractions, from the U.S. Air Force Academy and Pro Rodeo Hall of Fame to the Royal Gorge and Manitou's rollicking Iron Springs Chateau Melodrama Dinner Theatre. The area is even the locus of the nation's

Crowds filled the Brown Palace Hotel lobby (right) to watch Denver's first telecast of baseball's World Series in October 1951. The atrium itself was a novelty when the hotel opened in 1892. Alameda Avenue, the road up the mountains to the city's Red Rocks Amphitheater, was nowhere near as crowded in 1940 (opposite) as it is today.

second-oldest automobile race—not around an oval or through the streets of town, but up Pikes Peak each July at average speeds of more than one hundred miles per hour.

Although the area was once derided as the "Great American Desert," Northeast Colorado provides better farmland and a surprising feast of sites worth a detour off the interstate. These include the old Fondis ghost town near Kiowa, a beautifully restored carousel and replica of an old frontier town in Burlington, a historic automobile repair shop in Julesburg, and an Overland Trail Museum in Sterling. The region's largest city, Greeley, is home to Historic Centennial Village, a complex of structures ranging from a primitive one-room schoolhouse to a Victorian homestead. Greeley also plays host to the Independence Stampede, the largest Fourth of July rodeo in the world.

Colorado is often painted as the economic engine of the "New West," a term that means different things to different people. It connotes an appreciation of the West's attributes beyond cowboy nostalgia, including its vast mineral resources and its beautiful but fragile environment. New West think tanks, magazines, and newsletters are exploring issues like the impact of Chinese immigrants on the region's economy, and the potential harm from timber companies' clear-cutting and citizens' journeys into the wilderness on off-road vehicles. Because it is high plains, mountains, and plateau in one, Colorado faces a variety of challenges, while keeping a watchful eye out for another energy bust or diminution of the good life from too much growth. For the time being, Colorado is a pleasant surprise, even for those who visit expecting a wonderful time. Its mountains are even more spectacular than imagined; its climate sunnier and drier, cooler in summer and warmer in winter; its sunrises and sunsets more inspiring; its cities more cultural, and more fun. Red—*colorado*—is the color of passion, an appropriate name for a place so alluring.

OVERLEAF: Denver's skyline exploded with skyscrapers in the 1970s during an oil-price boom. Then many buildings fell half-empty in the bust to follow. Thanks in part to a surprising federal presence— Denver trails only Washington in the number of U.S. government employees—and to the arrival of several small high-tech firms, Denver occupancy figures strengthened again in the 1990s.

Denver's civic center is not a building but a huge, beautifully landscaped park that even contains a Greek amphitheater used for concerts. To one side of the flower-and statue-filled mall is the big City-County Building (opposite), also Greek in architectural influence. The gold-domed Colorado State Capitol (left), built on land donated by Henry C. Brown, owner of the Brown Palace Hotel, was deliberately constructed from materials quarried in Colorado. These included marble from the mountain town of the same name, granite from Gunnison, and all the world's supply of rose onyx, mined near the little town of Beulah. High on a hill, the Capitol affords a spectacular view of both downtown and the Front Range of the Rocky Mountains.

The Victorian parlor of the Molly Brown House and Museum (above) reflects the opulent standards of Denver's Pennsylvania Street. Molly and J. J. Brown bought the mansion after J. J. struck it rich in mines west of town. She thrived in—and he was chafed by— Denver's high society. The efforts to save Molly's Denver house led to the creation of Historic Denver, Incorporated, Denver's leading preservation organization. Balconies in the Brown Palace Hotel (opposite) rise eight floors above the ground. Two of the many panels of ornate grill-work were, perhaps purposely, installed upside down! Legend has it that a rail-car tunnel connected the hotel with a house of gambling and prostitution— now the Museum of Western Art—across the street. There is no evidence of this at the Brown Palace, but subterranean tracks, ending at a brick wall, were found beneath the museum.

Alexander Phimister Proctor's Broncho Buster *statue is a fixture in Denver's Civic Center park. And Proctor's* Bucking Bronco, *the rear piece among the four pictured (left), at the Museum of Western Art, continues the popular Colorado theme of taming both livestock and the West. The remaining bronzes in this gallery (opposite)—The* Cheyenne, Bronco Buster (Wooly Chaps), *and* Bronco Buster—*are by an even better-known artist, Frederic S. Remington. Little wonder the Denver football team was named the Broncos! The Museum of Western Art is located in downtown Denver's Navarre Building, once a bordello and gambling parlor. At the Denver Art Museum, a Spanish colonial gallery (above) is featured, along with stunning Asian and pre-Columbian exhibits and a changing selection of European masterpieces.*

The diverse Denver Botanic Gardens are located in tranquil Cheesman Park (left). The gardens depict: a transition zone between the Colorado plains and the Rocky Mountains' peaks; Shofu-en, *a Japanese Garden of Pine Wind;* a xeriscape display of plants from arid lands; a water plant collection; a nationally renowned alpine rock garden; a home-demonstration garden; and an area set aside for the conservation of endangered plants. Among the array of arresting exhibits at the Denver Museum of Natural History is the Rhodochrosite (above), a vivid Colorado gem found in pockets of granite. This specimen, the largest and finest ever unearthed, was discovered in 1992 at the Alma Mine in Park County.

The futuristic terminal at DIA, Denver's International Airport (above), suggests snow-capped Rocky Mountain peaks, but is located in the flatlands east of the city. Many open spaces within the *terminal are decorated with imaginative public art. In part because of the location's susceptibility to downdrafts coming off the Front Range of the Rockies, DIA has the world's most sophisti-* *cated airport facilities for predicting weather and dealing with adverse conditions. The Denver Center for the Performing Arts, downtown (opposite), turned frowsy old Curtis* *Street into an incredible arcade of theaters. Early in the twentieth century, more than ten thousand lights illuminated Curtis Street's thirteen legitimate theaters. The glow from their* *marquees could be seen far out on the prairie. The center is now a showcase for live theater, a nurturing ground for new plays, and a national training school for actors.*

To blend with natural mountain settings, Colorado landscapers often prefer a wild-flower garden (above) to formal plantings. This home is near Boulder on the outskirts of Denver.
In a state known for resorts, the Colorado Chautauqua (right) in Boulder is an anti-resort. Since 1897, people have come here to the base of the Flatiron Range for peace and quiet, hikes in the mountains, concerts, and inspirational oratory. In 1924, the peak year for chautauquas nationwide, one-third of the American population participated. But the Depression and the advent of movies and radio decimated the movement. The Colorado Chautauqua is a rare survivor.

Owners of outdoor pavilions often accentuate natural settings to enhance the concert experience. That's not necessary at the Red Rocks Amphitheater (opposite), high above Denver. Weathered red rocks provide a magnificent overlook of both the stage and the distant city skyline, and the acoustics are spectacular. The amphitheater was carved out of Mount Morrison's foothills by Civilian Conservation Corps workers from 1936 to 1941. William F. "Buffalo Bill" Cody was a man of all the West, but he died in Colorado while visiting his sister in Denver. He is buried on Lookout Mountain (left) on the grounds of the city-run Buffalo Bill Memorial Museum, which honors the exuberant scout and showman with guns, outfits, photos, and posters from his Pony Express and Wild West Show days.

It was not Horace Greeley—who popularized the phrase "Go west, young man"—but his agriculture editor at the New York Tribune, Nathan Meeker, who spearheaded a colonization effort in a town called Greeley in the "Great American Desert" for "ambitious individuals with high moral standards." Greeley today features churches like Nuestra Señora de la Paz (above), which conducts Masses in Spanish and English. Greeley's Centennial Village Museum (right) contrasts the harsh reality of pioneer life with the elegant beauty of the romantic Victorian era. Home of the University of Northern Colorado, Greeley hosts two of the region's largest festivals: an arts picnic, and the Cinco de Mayo/Semana Latina outdoor fiesta. But this is still farm and cattle-ranch country (opposite).

Cowboys like Woody White (opposite) are workaday fixtures, both on the range and in regional rodeos, in Northeast Colorado. This was the setting for James Michener's epic novel Centen-nial. *Huge cattle feed lots (above) are found in nearly every town on this great ocean of land. Colorado's outback—or, as locals like to call it, the "Other Colorado"— once the site of fierce Indian wars, is a place of limitless horizons, endless national grasslands, pioneer trails, mysterious caves— and great hunting for quail, deer, antelope, and bargain antiques. The Dust Bowl of the 1930s hit hard on Colorado's high plains, turning many communities into ghost towns. Those that remain increas-ingly rely on "cultural tourism." Julesburg, the "Wickedest City in the West" and Colorado's only Pony Express station stop, for instance, was the site of Fort Sedgwick, depicted in the hit movie* Dances With Wolves.

Burlington is a key city in "Coneka," where eastern Colorado, northwest Kansas, and southwest Nebraska meet. Its Kit Carson County Carousel (top right) was built in 1905 in Philadelphia for Denver's Elitch Gardens amusement park. When it was replaced there in 1928, this ornate creation was moved to Burlington. The ride was closed during the Depression, corn was stored around it, and rats damaged the carousel, Wurlitzer organ, and oil paintings. The magnificent carousel was restored in 1976 as a Bicentennial project and has been refurbished by local volunteers every summer since. Burlington's Old Town (bottom right) is a collection of twenty authentically remodeled historic buildings and turn-of-the-century artifacts. Even individual families try western decorative touches, as in this mailbox (opposite) near Rocky Ford.

Railroads, following the old Santa Fe Trail, were the lifeblood of Southeastern Colorado. Towns literally thrived or died, depending upon whether they enticed a railroad to lay tracks there. On the endless prairie, the rails seem to stretch forever (opposite). The town of La Junta is a key Santa Fe Railroad switching point (above). Coal and oil-shale petroleum from the mountains and agricultural products from the Colorado plains head east, and finished goods travel west. In today's computerized world, every boxcar and coal hopper is encoded with a bar code similar to those used on grocery-store products, and tracked by trackside scanners and satellites, mile by mile, from its origin to its destination. Shippers can follow the progress of their goods, and dispatchers in switching yards like this can quickly reshuffle the makeup of individual trains as they cross the country.

A sea of wild barley (above) lines U.S. Highway 350—the Kit Carson Trail—near the Kansas border in Southeastern Colorado. (Carson was a scout and Indian mediator who commanded Fort Garland, Colorado's first American military post, in the Sangre de Cristo Mountains. He deplored the massacres of defenseless Indian women and children in "battles" like the Sand Creek Reservation raid in 1864. Today there's a Carson museum in Las Animas.) In their crop rotation programs, farmers leave these fields alone for up to five years, helping to replenish nutrients in the soil. Then they bale this grain for their farm animals. Even more beautiful—and just as profitable a cash crop—are sunflowers (opposite); their seeds have become one of America's favorite snack foods. Agricultural products alone account for more than $800,000 in Colorado's annual foreign exports.

One day in 1995, an itinerant Guatemalan artist, Carlos Silva, showed up in the little ranching town of La Veta at the base of the Sangre de Cristo Mountains' Spanish Peaks, offering to paint murals. In return, he asked only for brushes, paint, and a meal or two. He found several takers, including the owner of an old cheese factory that was being converted from a storage building into apartments. This memorable mural (opposite) was the result. Silva moved on to do other work in Walsenburg, Trinidad, and who knows where else. In the "middle of nowhere," across the railroad tracks from the tiny settlement of Tyrone in Las Animas County, stands an abandoned adobe one-room schoolhouse (above). For many years, one teacher taught almost one hundred students—kindergartners through eighth-graders—in this little building. It is now a warehouse.

Bent's Old Fort (left), near La Junta, was a privately owned trading post on the Santa Fe Trail in the mid-nineteenth century. The "Castle of the Plains" was a post where Americans, French, Mexicans, and peaceful Plains Indians traded beaver pelts, buffalo hides, mules, blankets, iron goods, and luxuries such as coffee and tobacco. The

Madonna of the Trail in Lamar (above) is one of twelve monuments sponsored by the Daughters of the American Revolution to mark old National Trails. The Madonna, depicting pioneer mothers in covered-wagon days, was located in Big Timbers, a forty-five-mile-long growth of cottonwood trees that provided refuge along the Arkansas River.

In Pueblo, named for the old El Pueblo trading post at a crossroads shared by five Native American tribes, the grandly restored Union Depot (top right) again shows off its mosaic tile flooring and richly polished wood wainscoting in corridors now used for offices and shops. As plans proceeded to build a San Antonio-style riverwalk shopping area, the row of mansions along Pitkin Avenue (bottom right) remained a tourist attraction. To the south in Walsenburg, the "City Built on Coal," the Mining Museum in an old county jail (opposite) tells the story of the coal camps, miners of twenty-six nationalities, and bitter strikes. One of Colorado's man-made wonders is the world's highest suspension bridge— the Royal Gorge Bridge in Cañon City (overleaf)— completed in 1929.

The mountains above Colorado Springs are a visual delight in all seasons (above), and the view of the valley below is spectacular. Behind the cluster of city buildings, the red rocks of the Garden of the Gods (right) jut up from the foothills. As moratoriums have been placed on development in the mountains, subdivisions have spread eastward onto the plains. Retired Civil War general William Jackson Palmer, president of the Denver & Rio Grande Railroad, laid out Colorado Springs as a resort, modeled after Tudor England. For years, the city was known as "Little London," and later, once a thriving arts community grew and wealthy businessmen built mansions, it was called the "Newport of the Rockies." The city is now one of the West's fastest-growing communities.

In 1870, William Jackson Palmer caught his first glimpse of the 14,000-foot-high Pikes Peak (left) beyond his new town that would become Colorado Springs. He later wrote his wife, "Could one live in constant view of these grand mountains without being elevated by them into a lofty plane of thought and purpose?" Pikes Peak is now the second-most visited mountain in the world, behind Japan's Mount Fuji. The Colorado Springs Pioneer Museum (above) is located in the old El Paso County Courthouse. One of the state's delightful attractions is the Historic Iron Springs Chateau melodrama (overleaf) in nearby Manitou Springs. There, audience members follow the piano player's lead in rooting for the hero and heroine and unmercifully hissing the dastardly villain.

The reading alcove of the 1895 Miramont Castle Museum (top right) in Manitou Springs is one restored element within the grand Victorian mansion. The castle, which was commissioned by French-born Catholic priest Jean Baptist Francolon as a home for himself and his widowed mother, includes an "International Museum of Miniatures" in the basement. An old-fashioned barber shop (below right) is one stop along Main Street in the Colorado Springs Ghost Town Museum, which was built from actual structures found abandoned and decaying in the mountains. In another room, visitors can swagger into an authentic saloon and step up to one of the region's first bars. The aristocratic Broadmoor resort (opposite), completed in 1918, includes thirty buildings and three championship golf courses.

The site of the Will Rogers Shrine to the Sun (right), high above the zoo on Cheyenne Mountain in Colorado Springs, was intended as a final resting place for Broadmoor Hotel entrepreneur Spencer Penrose and his wife, Julie. But when Penrose's famous friend was killed in a plane crash in 1937, the memorial was built and dedicated to Rogers. Interior walls are covered with painted western scenes and photographs and aphorisms of the cowboy philosopher. The seventeen aluminum, glass, and steel spires of the Cadet Chapel of the United States Air Force Academy (opposite) soar one hundred fifty feet toward the sky. The building contains separate chapels for Protestant, Catholic, and Jewish cadets and visitors, as well as an all-faiths room for other worshipers.

Red rocks in the Garden of the Gods, near Colorado Springs, can take on a dozen hues in the same day, depending upon the intensity and angle of light. The free park, a gift to the city by the family of railroad baron Charles Perkins in 1909, has the feel of a lunar landscape. Its loop road winds past jutting red sandstone formations—including a bizarre balanced rock—and Colorado's largest trading post. At the visitor center, tourists can view a multimedia show that describes the area's intriguing geological history. It's thought that beautiful Colorado's most photographed scene is Pikes Peak, framed between the park's Gateway Rocks.

Tour buses from Denver pass through Clear Creek Canyon (opposite) on their way to the casinos of Central City (above), one of three Colorado towns where gambling has been legalized. Black Hawk, just down U.S. Route 6, and Cripple Creek, west of Colorado Springs, are the others. In Central City, all kinds of indigenous buildings—even gas stations—have been converted into small casinos. In its gold-rush days, this was "The Richest Square Mile on Earth." Among its attractions today is the Gilpin County Historical Society Museum, open from May through September and by appointment the other months. It features mining displays, a doll and toy exhibit, and a vintage-1869 clothing collection. A gem amid the clutter in Black Hawk, where much of Central City's ore was once smelted, is a delicate Victorian "Lace House," now also a museum.

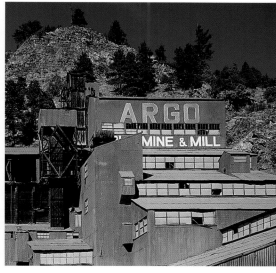

Scenic Georgetown's Victorian shopping district (left) and Georgetown Loop Railroad—built by financier Jay Gould as a spur to the gold mines for his Colorado Central Railroad— are tourist magnets. Visitors can still ride the narrow-gauge, steam-powered train over the awe-inspiring Devil's Gate Bridge— called "The Eighth Wonder of the World" when it was completed in 1888. The huge Argo gold mill in Idaho Springs (above), now a mining museum, offers tours through the long Newhouse Tunnel back into an old mine. A more natural attraction, still higher in the mountains, is the spectacular Dillon Reservoir (overleaf), a boaters' paradise and the state's largest body of water. An entire small town and many square miles of valley land were sub- merged to create it.

The beauty of Colorado's Rocky Mountains is accentuated when snow covers the soaring peaks. Above Loveland Pass on the Continental Divide—13,900 feet high—inveterate skier Carol Brownson, owner of the Ridge Street Inn in Breckenridge, glides in splendid isolation (opposite). Utes once trapped beaver here, keeping the presence of gold secret from whites for fifty years before the veins were discovered and the Indians driven out. The mountains near Dillon (above) are a sightseeing and hiking fairyland. In the summertime, herds of elk move up beyond the timberline to graze in high pastures. Lichen clings to rocks year-round, and each summer wildflowers turn high valleys into bonanzas of color. Skiing is big business on the peaks above Breckenridge (overleaf), which enjoyed earlier prosperity as a silver boomtown after a barber noted the flecks of silver in a customer's hair.

Leadville, high in the
Central Rockies, has
a rich history in more
ways than one. The
discovery of silver
swelled its population
to fifty thousand in
the 1870s. Horace
Tabor, whose Match-
less silver mine made
him a multimillion-
aire, built a beautiful
opera house (right).
Hotels like the
Delaware (above),
restored in the 1990s,
once catered to a
wealthy if eccentric
clientele. So dilet-
tantish was life
in Leadville for a
while that residents
found time to build a
five-acre ice palace,
complete with statues,
in the winter of
1895–96. The carefree
days are recalled in
artist F. F. Haberlein's
mural (overleaf), pro-
moting the book and
play Leadville USA.

Colorado's cattle ranching is not confined to the eastern plains. Even high in the mountains north of Granite (left), ranchers make the most of available meadows. Below the treeline along the Continental Divide in the Sawatch Range, conifers (above) blanket the mountainsides in green. This is windy and often foggy terrain. Rainy, too, and so snowy in winter that many high-mountain passes must be closed as early as September and as late as April. The rainfall feeds reservoirs that provide water to Front Range cities like Denver and Fort Collins, and mountain snows make for world-class skiing conditions. Above the timberline on the state's tallest peaks, permanently frozen subsoil, called permafrost, extends to a depth of one hundred feet or more.

In Colorado's long winters, the two-hundred-mile-wide Rocky Mountains were a formidable, often deadly, barrier to American westward expansion—and to Spanish and Mexican migration north of Santa Fe. Until the discovery of gold and the development of mechanized travel, only Indians and "mountain men" trappers ventured into the Rockies.

Most trails from Missouri veered north into tamer passes in Wyoming or south into New Mexico, and wagon masters who tried to push a caravan through the Rockies carefully timed their journeys to arrive at Colorado's Front Range in springtime. To this day, avalanches are such a threat that the state highway department builds reinforced sheds over portions of some mountain passes to deflect the slides. While the roads are closed, it also deliberately sets off avalanches to prevent catastrophes when cars, trucks, and buses pass later.

Olsen's Cabins at Twin Lakes (above) on Colorado Route 82, the road through Independence Pass to Aspen, hark back to simpler days of family travel. Twin Lakes was a rest stop for stagecoaches from Leadville to towns to the west in what is now the San Isabel National Forest. The old gold-mining camp called Independence, east of Aspen, is today a ghost town. At almost thirteen thousand feet, Independence Pass (opposite) through the Sawatch Range is the highest crossing of the Continental Divide. It is closed in winter and at other times when blinding snowstorms hit. The view of the timberline from the tundra at the pass's summit (overleaf) truly suggests the top of the world. Here, underpowered automobiles as well as hikers are quickly affected by the High Country's long inclines and thin air.

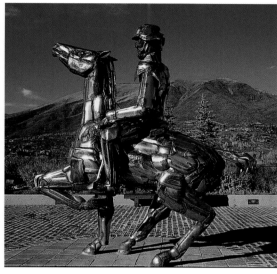

Aspen is a world-famous ski destination, and the town is a fashionable enclave of celebrities' chalets, gourmet restaurants, and art museums. Chicago industrialist Walter Paepcke's "Aspen idea"—making a good living while enjoying art, music, and films—germinated here. One of Colorado's oldest and grandest buildings is Aspen's Pitkin County Courthouse (left), completed in 1891. A silver statue of Justice, crafted in Ohio, was installed—minus the customary blindfold—above the main entrance. In 1977, mass murderer Ted Bundy escaped from this courthouse during his trial. Popular "bumper art" (above), crafted from automobile bumpers by Aspen's Lou Wille, can be found in several Colorado towns. Aspens in McClure Pass (overleaf), one valley over from the town of Aspen, deliver a spectacular fall show.

The rushing Crystal River (opposite), between Aspen and Carbondale, is a favorite haunt for trout fishers, and the surrounding stands of aspens and birch (left and above) double the pleasure each autumn. Cleveholm Manor (overleaf) in tiny Redstone, west of Aspen, was built by benevolent industrialist Cleve Osgood and his Swedish-born second wife, Alma (hence the holm, Swedish for "home"). Osgood, who owned a big steel mill in Pueblo, set up an American feudal kingdom in Redstone, where his coke workers lived in eighty-four frame cottages and a bachelors' inn. Families enjoyed full access to the town's schoolhouse, recreation center, and library—but almost never Cleveholm itself.

Cleve Osgood, the
"Lion of Redstone,"
and his wife, Alma,
traveled the world
and accumulated
treasures for Cleve-
holm Castle. Writer
Martie Sterling
described the red-
sandstone castle as
"a transmogrified
Hudson River manor
with overtones of King
Ludwig," replete with
trophy heads, Tiffany
lamps, ruby velvet
drapes, Russian
dinner service, and
Moroccan leather wall
coverings. Osgood
moved to New York,
bought a city block
and built a house on
it, and hobnobbed
with other capital-
ists—often inviting
them to ride his
private railroad car
to Redstone for a
summer's visit. Even-
tually he divorced
Alma to marry a
twenty-year-old
former chorus girl.
After his death, Cleve-
holm became a dude
ranch house, then a
resort hotel. Since
restored, it is now a
delightful bed-and-
breakfast inn.

The scenery in the canyon country of Northwest Colorado is indistinguishable from rockbound Utah. Ranches like this spread (left), beneath Book Cliffs near the town of Whitewater, often have vast reaches of the scrubby high desert (above) to themselves. Because of the arid soil, cattle must range over wide territory to scrounge both meals and water. Erosion has worn down boulders that pushed through the earth's crust in the cataclysmic grinding of tectonic plates millions of years ago. This is lizard, rattlesnake, and mountain lion country—rich in hidden dinosaur bones from an era when this land was lush with vegetation. Here, evergreens quickly yield to sagebrush and oak chaparral. Much of the land north and west of Grand Junction is federal land, pocked with mineral mines.

Grand Junction, Colorado's western gateway—named for the confluence of the Colorado and Gunnison rivers—is the base camp for adventures through sandstone canyons, deserts, and even sprawling peach orchards. One sees lots of "Hawgs" on the desolate highways, and inside the Harley-Davidson dealership in town (above) there's an old-fashioned diner, moved from New Jersey. Horses (right) may soon be outnumbered by off-road vehicles in the rugged region. In the Grand Valley of the Colorado River is Colorado National Monument (overleaf), not a single structure but a twenty-thousand-acre maze of arched rock windows, spires, and monoliths. In the distance is the tiny town of Fruita. Nearby is Grand Mesa—the largest flat-topped "island in the sky" in the world.

Colorado's high desert (above) is Valhalla for rock hounds. There's a daunting "Trail Through Time" over outcroppings in Rabbit Valley (opposite), along the road to Dinosaur National Monument in the northwestern corner of the state. The trail, administered by the U.S. Bureau of Land Management and the Museum of Western Colorado, leads past plant fossils, ancient stream channels, greenish prehistoric mudstones, and locations where dinosaurs like Diplodocus, Iguanodon, and Camarasaurus were excavated. Some bones remain visible, embedded in boulders. Others are exhibited at the Museum of Western Colorado in Grand Junction. And at the Devils Canyon Science & Learning Center in Fruita, visitors encounter life-size robotic dinosaurs, and earthquake simulator, and hands-on interactive exhibits about area geology. South of Grand Junction, heading back into higher country, the Gunnison River (overleaf) begins as a trickle. Not far downstream, however, it rages.

One can hear the roar of the rushing water far below, and sense its tremendous power, above the steep, dark Black Canyon of the Gunnison River (opposite) near Montrose. Geologist Wallace Hansen wrote that "no other canyon in North America combines the depth, narrowness, sheerness, and somber countenance of the Black Canyon of the Gunnison." The landscape above the canyon (above), however, is anything but black. Several Spanish and American expeditions—including one led by Captain John W. Gunnison himself in the 1860s— trudged right past the narrow gorge without spotting it. To the south, in the Dolores River Valley (overleaf), aspens make another fall appearance. The trees' delicate yellow or gold leaves may not match the Northeast's splendor in variety of hue, but their translucent shimmering in the crisp mountain breezes is an unforgettable show of its own.

Cliff Harding raises llamas at his ranch near Hotchkiss (left). Individual buyers purchase the South American pack animals, which can carry about seventy pounds of goods and travel up to ten miles a day, as sure-footed back-country beasts of burden. The gentle, clean animals are prized for their wool and make curious pets. Llamas spit at each other, hum to their young, and give off high-pitched screams when threatened. Telluride, the nineteenth-century mining town in a box canyon below Bridal Veil Falls, is a ski resort and a fascinating combination of old and new—sometimes in the same buildings (above). Like the northwestern part of the state, Southwestern Colorado has its windswept deserts (overleaf), but they are somewhat more verdant and colorful.

Mesa Verde Indians abandoned their mesa-top pueblos (above) for more defensible positions in caves and hollows in cliff ledges about A.D. 1200. Cliff Palace (left) had twenty-three underground kivas—ceremonial rooms—and enough dwelling rooms for about two hundred people. These "ancient ones" maintained their fields of corn, beans, and squash atop the mesa, reached by hand- and toeholds cut into the cliffs. Probably due to drought rather than enemy threats, they deserted these dwellings after only seventy-five or so years. It is thought that they headed south, across the rugged terrain beneath Mesa Verde (overleaf), and were absorbed into other tribes.

119

Oversized tepees and arrows at The Hogan Indian arts and crafts post in Mancos (opposite) serve as can't-miss roadside billboards for the clothing and trinkets for sale inside.

Genuine Indian and Spanish rugs are popular in Southwestern Colorado as well. The La Unica Cosa gallery in Durango (above)—in a building that was once a grocery store on lively Main Avenue— boasts, along with its outlet in Taos, New Mexico, the world's largest collection of Zapotec Indian weavings. Although many ranches in the San Juan Mountain valleys around Durango were turned into lovely bed-and-breakfast inn sites, the town's main street was an eyesore until concerted civic action remade it into a vibrant promenade of restaurants, boutiques, and renovated hotels. The Animas Museum, downtown, details Durango's colorful history as a railroad town and supplier to the region's gold camps.

An estimated $300 million in precious metals was carried down from mines of the San Juan Mountains to Animas City (now Durango). Today, tourists retrace the route through Ute Indian country aboard cars of the coal-fired Durango & Silverton Railroad (left). Along the way, backpackers, fishermen, and hikers may hop off at two flag stops. Cowboy humorist Will Rogers and western novelist Louis L'Amour were two long-term guests of the Strater Hotel (above), since restored, in Durango. Great Sand Dunes National Monument (overleaf), nearly seven hundred feet high and forty square miles in scope, was formed when fierce winds off the desert piled sand at the base of the Sangre de Cristo Mountains. The dunes' size and shape changes slightly with each strong wind.

Index

Meadows are serene
on the Zapata Ranch
near Mosca, north
of Alamosa on the edge
of San Luis Lakes State
Park. The Zapata is
now a resort, where
golfers tee off next to
herds of domesticated
bison. Restaurants,
like the legendary
Buckhorn Exchange
in Denver, tout the
leanness of buffalo
steaks and burgers.